Reduce, Reuse and Recycle

Optimize Your Marketing

Jennifer de Spain

Timothy Robertson

ISBN: 0692526595
ISBN-13: 978-0692526590

www.ingramcontent.com/pod-product-compliance
Lightning Source LLC
Chambersburg PA
CBHW070826210326
41520CB00011B/2129

DEDICATIONS

My contributions in this book are dedicated to the life and loving memory of my grandpa, the most brilliant and kindest man I have ever met.

-Jennifer de Spain

To my dad, who never fails to be supportive when it counts most.

-Timothy Robertson

CONTENTS

ACKNOWLEDGMENTS

We would like to thank

Mel Cutler for providing our foreword,
Larry Walker for designing the cover art, and
Miguel Lopez and Stephany Ocampo for transcription.

FOREWORD

Whether you are a seasoned entrepreneur or are just starting out on the journey, it is no secret that being able to optimize your marketing is crucial to your success now and in the future.

Since I have experienced the proverbial ups and downs that come with sailing the seas of entrepreneurship, I know how to spot a top-notch lighthouse who knows marketing the way Jennifer de Spain does to guide you to your destined shore of success.

Her book *Reduce, Reuse, and Recycle: Optimize Your Marketing* is your entrepreneurial marketing map to providing you with the strategies to get you there.

No matter if you are someone who has an existing business and need to market yourself to increase your business or if you are currently employed by a company and are considering venturing out on your own, the truth be known that there are no guarantees in our economic environment today—except the guarantee that if you position yourself well and target your message in various ways through reducing, reusing, and recycling it to the right audiences in a way that solves their pain and delivers on your promise, it significantly ups your chances of achieving the success you want and deserve.

You do not have to look far to see that today's economic tides have changed in a way that impacts companies and people within them. It is undeniable that…

- People no longer find security in their jobs or count on them to provide for retirement.
- People need more money to sustain them over their longer life spans.
- People want joy and happiness to be an integral part of their work.

- Companies send jobs overseas to reduce costs and increase profits.
- Companies go out of business more now than ever.
- Companies are no longer granted the blanket trust people used to have in them.

Rather than leave you on a down note with these facts, I want you to notice as you read de Spain's book that hope rises within you like the sun on the horizon. As an entrepreneur, you owe it to yourself to invest in your business so you profit more to turn the tides in your direction.

Here's what I undoubtedly recommend:

- Read this book
- Take notes
- Create a marketing plan
- Prepare for increased business (and income!)
- Take massive action

Even though the seas may be rough at first (and quite possibly at various times), having the tools of effective marketing will give you confidence to know that with the right optimized marketing actions you can steer and direct your sails to rise above and succeed.

Bon voyage!

Mel Ethan Cutler
Founder, Success Academy
Author, *Big Boom!* book
BigBoombook.com

PART ONE: REDUCE

Whether you measure value in time, money or manpower, your business is expensive. However, when you empower yourself with the right tools and leverage those tools you are opening doors to new opportunities. By leveraging the tools available to you, you begin to reduce the time, money and manpower your business needs while increasing the effectiveness of your marketing.

This is powerful as marketing is your company's only method of attracting new customers. When you can create more effective marketing for less time, money and manpower, your business can thrive and prosper.

This section of reduce, reuse and recycle is dedicated to providing you with a road map to effective and efficient marketing. We will delve into automation, search engine optimization, when to spend money and much more. You are provided with powerful resources that can change the way you look at marketing.

Are you ready for a change of perspective?

Let's get started!

TIME

Reducing the time you spend on your marketing without sacrificing the quality of your marketing is one of the most important things you can do to improve your business. It saves you the one and only commodity you can never get back: your precious time.

Save time with your business and be careful not to cut corners in the process. Your business depends on marketing to survive and taking shortcuts can be disastrous. This has been proven again and again by each and every failed company. However, take the advice in this section and you will find the efficiency of your business improve and your marketing abilities soaring to new heights. Let's begin now!

Automation, Automation, Automation!

One way to reduce the time you spend on your marketing process is to implement systems. Marketing is often pushed off by business owners to make room for necessary tasks like bookkeeping and working on the services and products provided by your company. Do yourself a favor and don't be that business owner.

Your business cannot run without marketing, as without marketing your company will not have any clients. Your business should be able to run without you. This is where systems come in. You can use systems to keep your business working, so you can work on your business by marketing.

An example of a system would be to create instructional videos to help new hires become familiar with the processes and the operations of your business instead of training each new hire individually. It'll take you a little more time to create instructional videos than it would for you to train one new hire, but when you consider that you may be training ten, twenty, one hundred, or even more new hires over the course of your business, this will save you a lot of time that you can use for your marketing campaign or other useful activities.

Another way you can save time in your marketing process is by using software that is designed to help you save time. Many different software have the capability to make complicated tasks as easy as pushing a button. Those are extremely valuable, so make sure that you can use those in your business to decrease the amount of time you have to spend. Remember, your time is money, and these software can help save you that time and money.

In addition, some software can automate tasks purely to save time. Not making tasks less complicated, but just speeding them up.

For example, some software allow you to post all your social media accounts from one page. Others allow you to log into multiple accounts to compare data. In fact, our new software, Introspect SEO, will be doing both of these tasks simultaneously to save you time.

Software like these save you time and keep you from spending all your time on marketing, so you don't have to push it off like the unfortunate business owner that's doing everything themselves.

A third way to save yourself time in your marketing plan is if you have a storefront that you are operating, add an online store front to your arsenal. This can help you in a number of ways but first and foremost, it allows your customers to purchase your product with these from any location. This means that even the laziest customer can select and purchase your product from their cell phone in bed with their pajamas on. This goes a long way toward building a lasting relationship with your customers and is a great way to market your storefront.

Additionally, it adds a new channel for your business to bring in revenue that, if you did not have an online storefront, you would not have had access to at all. This will help your company thrive over time.

Organizing Your Day

So let's talk about organizing your day properly. You first off have to have a mindset that allows you to work. So what does that mean? When you have a bad mindset, it's limiting beliefs. Thoughts like "oh, I can't do this," "oh I can't do that," "it's too hard," "I don't want to do that" are limiting beliefs. These are beliefs that are going to keep you from getting your tasks done. So change your mindset. There are different techniques to do that.

First and foremost, set official working hours. When you are an entrepreneur, or a business owner, or even a CEO, we all tend work over hours, we try to be flexible and we feel that's part of customer service. Well it's not. Being an on-call doctor does not make you more valuable, it actually makes you less valuable because your customer does not respect you when you are an on call doctor. They have business hours, so you can give yourself business hours and that is perfectly reasonable.

My recommendation, and what I did for myself, was I said 9 to 5, Monday through Friday and then if there was something that went over that, that's where I said "hey, you are so valuable to me that I'm going to work overtime for you." It not only gives you the ability to pull back for yourself, but it also gives you something to fall back on when there is a project where you're going "Hey, I'm tired, I need to go and be with my family," and people respect that. It will make you look like you really truly care when you do overtime.

And of course you do care. This isn't a fake thing; this is you giving an environment to your customer that will entice them to work with you.

So give yourself official working hours. Put them in your in your signature on your emails. Put it on your business cards. Put them on your website. Make sure that people know what your limitations are and then exceed those when appropriate. It will help you sleep better give yourself time before going to bed. Now you work and work and work and you're writing your last email, you're sitting in your bed, you turn off your phone and try to go to sleep. I guarantee you you're not going to wake up well rested. You are going to wake up very tired thinking about what your email was. Put your phone down, put your computer to sleep on time. That's going to help you out significantly.

That will help people respect you, which is even more important. Be realistic about how much you plan for yourself in a day. We all have those lists that are never ending. That does not mean that you should be able to get them done all in one day. Plan out your day and double the time that you estimate each task will take.

I'm serious about this, if you say something is going to take you 10 minutes, put it down for 20, or maybe even 30. Something's going to take half an hour? Set an hour. Make sure that you give yourself lunch, and put that on your schedule "Make Sure I Eat Lunch."

We all have interruptions. We all have people calling out of the blue. We all have these emergency projects that come up. We all have dogs that run into the room, kids to run into the room, emergency drives to the vet. We all have things happen to us no matter where we are, or what position we have. Whether we own a business, or we work at McDonalds. So plan for those occurrences.

Map out your day and make sure that you give a good amount of time for interruption because they just happen. That's how you can you can really make yourself feel good about the work you're doing also, because when you put too much on your list and you can get them done you feel really bad about yourself.

That does not make for a happy worker. You're not going to be happy doing your work when you feel like you can't get anything done. Don't put that pressure on yourself because it will show and it will trickle down to other people and that's not going to be good for them either. So make sure that you're reasonable with yourself and schedule appropriately. One way you can do that is by doubling the time that you estimate things will take.

When you get your tasks done early it will make you feel wonderful. When you can get everything on your list done by the end of the day and you can leave early, you are going to be jumping for joy! You're going to be happy going to bed because you're well rested since you gave yourself working hours and time to relax. The next morning, you're going to have a fresh list of things to do, and people are going to be happy with you because you're not over promising.

Take it upon yourself to be really be realistic with what you expect from yourself. When you write out your list, double the time and don't put too much. Just as an exercise one day, put 5 items on your to-do list: three in the morning, two in the afternoon. See how that works out for you. If you can add more in then do so. If it's way too much and you have really huge task that you're taking on, cut it down to four. Whatever it takes, just make sure that you are giving yourself enough time to get your tasks done.

Overworking yourself does not mean you're super dedicated, it just means that you don't respect yourself enough to give yourself a break. So, start respecting yourself and give yourself back your time!

Outsource to Professionals

Here's another tip: hire someone else to do the things you don't want to or can't do. Hire an expert in the field. They are going to be fast. This is EXTREMELY beneficial to your business.

For example, let's say there's a there's a business owner who needs a website. There are free tools out there, but they're not going to get the result they need because they're not experienced in it, so they would hire a company like mine because we know what we're doing and we can get it done fast.

Do something like that. Let's say you're doing the accounting for your business. If you don't like numbers, don't do the accounting. Instead, hire a CPA.

Taxes. You don't want to do taxes. That's perfectly fine, go to HR Block or any number of places. Private tax consultants will do your taxes too and it's an alternative to TurboTax, which you do yourself.

Pass it along to someone else and pay them to do it right. Not only is it a time saver, but it will end up saving you money later down the road. Remember, there's a little bit of an overlap between the Time section of the Money section of your business because Time IS Money. So the more time you are spending doing things that you're not an expert in, the more money you are losing because you are not doing the job that you love.

Have someone else do the things you don't want to do. It's as simple as that. It's worth the money, they're going to be fast, and you can do something else at the same time.

Okay, one more bonus, because this one's huge. Get a business lawyer to review all of your contracts. Let me repeat that, GET A BUSINESS LAWYER to review and/or write all of your contracts. One more time, get a business lawyer to review and/or write ALL of your contracts.

This is extraordinarily important, don't try to write your own contract. Remember, lawyers are trained to work with the government and what the government allows to happen and does not allow to happen. Your contracts are a reflection of what the government will allow you to do. They are extensions of it.

Let's say you have an employee. Well, your employee has to abide by certain guidelines set forth by a contract, but if you write it yourself there's going to be a loophole in there. I'm not saying maybe. There WILL be something in there that IS a loophole that your employee will be able to worm around and you're going to get a lot of money taken from you, when it's really not your fault. Your employee could be dead wrong and because of the one slip up on one line and one word you will lose a lot of money.

That is the power of having a business lawyer do it. Make sure it's not just a general lawyer, it has to be a BUSINESS lawyer. When you have a business lawyer look over your contract make sure they understand what your vision is for your business. A GOOD lawyer will incorporate your vision and make sure that the values that are important to you are covered.

So, for me, I always want to make sure that my clients are equally covered as much as I, so I don't give contracts that only cover me. My lawyer understood that and he made sure that the contracts he wrote aligned with my vision of how I wanted to do business.

Be certain that you have somebody who understands you and will work with you to make sure that if there's something that you're doing that may not fit quite right with your vision, they will tell you.

They aren't just mercenaries looking for the money. They will actually tell you, and there are lawyers out there like that. Trust me, my lawyer is awesome!

Leverage other people's time. This one is also extraordinarily important. Don't try to do everything yourself.

You can be a jack of all trades that's wonderful, you should know a little bit of everything, but knowing a little bit of everything does not mean that you should be *doing* everything. What is actually means is that you have the ability to manage people who do the things you know about to your standards!

As an employee or contractor is doing the low hanging fruit, a.k.a. work, like cutting up wood or some other basic task, you can be talking to the client at the same time. You are having one of your contractors or your employees go over and cut up the wood. See how much time you can save?

That's how you can leverage other people's time. Hiring someone to handle low-handing fruit overlaps with hiring an expert in the field that leverage *their* time, and as a result you're able to charge for that time at your rate. Does that make sense?

Charge for someone else's time at your rate. So you have that contractor here cutting up wood and they charge you $20 an hour. Well, your rate is $50 or maybe even $100. To your clients you're charging for your time, meanwhile you're able to do other things and get other projects done for them making it much faster to get the overall project done and it is more cost efficient for you. It's not just "okay, well I'm working on project for an hour... $100 for me... and then my contractor work for an hour... so, $20 for him." No. That's $200 because you're charging his time, YOUR rate. That's much more efficient, much easier to keep track of and is extraordinarily legitimate.

This is common practice this is not cheap skate stuff. This is not slimy. This is how it's done. This is how you can efficiently get tasks done for yourself and get compensated well for it.

Give it a try and let me know how it works for you!

"The man who stops advertising to save money is like the man who stops the clock to save time."
-Thomas Jefferson

MONEY

It's imperative that you reduce the money you spend efficiently in order to have a successful business. Here we cover simple ways that you can save money so that you can invest it in the appropriate places in your business.

Give yourself *time* freedom and *mind* freedom by letting go of the inefficient costly software and saying hello to the simple solutions.

You know that reducing money being spent in your business is important. Now let's talk about ways that we can do that!

Use Free or Inexpensive Software

First off, research free or inexpensive alternatives to spendy software. Three of the largest expenses that you can have in your marketing could be your mass mailing, your analytics data, and your video productions.

Those are the three main components that are going to suck up most of your money. Let's begin with mass mailing.

Mass Mailing

Many mass mailing programs cost per email or per contact, so, for example, you can get 2000 contacts, but after that point you have to spend $20 per month just to have those contacts, or you can be charged per email.

That can add up - QUICKLY. If you are doing well in your business you're going to quickly start spending hundreds and hundreds of dollars per month on your emails alone. Now that doesn't make a lot of sense to me especially when you have free alternatives such as AcyMailing, which is a plugin, that can be used with the Joomla content management system (which is a wonderful system for building websites).

Google Analytics

Another software that's helpful for reducing your overhead in your marketing campaign is Google Analytics.

There are a lot of very expensive software out there that will help you analyze the traffic coming to your website, and get usable data from it so that you can structure your marketing campaign. The free alternative to these is Google Analytics.

All you have to do to get Google Analytics setup is install one simple code in your website. Once you do this you can track seemingly unlimited kinds of data using Google Analytics: everything from how many times your page has been viewed, to how many users are on your website, to what location they're actually viewing your site from.

So let's suppose you have a massive following in Uganda. Google Analytics would display that your audience is mainly from Uganda, with some statistics when and how those users get to your site. However, if you wanted your main audience to be mostly from the United States, it would allow you to find information that you use to shift the focus of your website so that you would get the audience you want.

YouTube and Production Software

Another Google product that's great for marketing is YouTube. YouTube allows you to publish videos for free and market them to millions of viewers worldwide.

An added benefit for using YouTube is Google's audio analysis system. Their analysis system listens to the audio on your video and will keep track of the key words that you say. So make sure when you use YouTube you speak very clearly and very smoothly. Google will be able to hear what you say and write it out.

Not only can that be used for the closed caption feature on your YouTube videos, but since YouTube is owned by Google, Google will use those keywords as part of your search engine optimization. You can use this to help direct traffic to your website.

For production of your videos, before they get to YouTube, consider cloud review and approval systems, such as www.ScreenLight.TV.

BONUS SYSTEM!

Here's a bonus system in addition to the three we just listed that will help you to reduce your costs in your marketing plan. Instead of using expensive systems such as Yelp to get your company's name out there to the general public, take advantage of **free** *social media* opportunities provided by Twitter, Facebook, and Pinterest to get attention to your name and your brand without spending money.

In addition to saving you money in your marketing plan this can also increase your brand loyalty, AND your brand power, AND your brand's value. This will help you gain a competitive edge over your competitors who may not be using these free software for same purposes.

Referencing back to saving time, you can easily have interns, volunteers or new employees managing your social media campaign so that you can spend your time doing the things you'd rather be doing.

Natural Google Results

One ways to reduce your costs in marketing is to get natural Google results instead of paid results. This is done through a process called search engine optimization, or SEO.

SEO

Search Engine Optimization costs a bit more than pay per click (PPC) ads up front, but in the long run it will save you a lot of time and money because you're not paying for every click through to your website as you would with pay per click ads.

There are three major components to SEO that you need to be aware of so that you can begin to implement them in your business and get the results you need!

1. Keyword Analysis

Keyword analysis allows you to find with the marketplace wants and cater your message to fulfill their needs and give them what they want. Your service or product should be geared toward an audience you want.

2. Code

The next part of SEO that you should be aware of is specialized coding on your website. You can integrate the keywords from your analysis into the code of your website so that search engines, when they read through your website, will find you relevant to the searcher's wants and needs. Examples of these codes are Meta Descriptions and MicroData. For more information on specialized code used for SEO, visit our blog: www.deSpaindeSigns.com/blog

CAUTION: Be very careful when you are implementing and tinkering with code on your website. If you are unfamiliar with the fundamental coding languages PHP and HTML, you should seek the advice or assistance of an experienced professional so as to avoid catastrophic damage to your website.

3. Authoritative Backlinks

The third part of SEO you need to know is configuring a web of authoritative backlinks to your product and brand.

This is not as simple as the other two aspects of SEO because it requires a third party. You have to ask third party companies to sponsor you or to feature your link on their website.

For example, if you are a local restaurant you may find an online local newspaper that reports and posts about events and happenings in your town. You can find that local online newspaper, then ask the newspaper to publish an article about your restaurant on their website.

This will not only bring in more traffic from the link but it will increase your status in Google and other search engines so that your website becomes more relevant to searchers.

Content Marketing

Another great way to save money on your marketing plan is to use a technique called content marketing. As with SEO, this can cost a little bit more in the beginning but will pay out more drastically as you progress.

The basic principle behind content marketing is that you're giving information away for free. Give your customers and your clients valuable information about your industry that they can use. This will positions you as an *expert* in your field and will make you stand out above your competition, who, often times, are just in it for the sale.

Your customers may not have a problem now, but when they do they will think of you first because you've been giving them valuable information that they can use to better their business on an everyday basis, AND you will end up getting the sale instead of your competitors.

One special form of content marketing is blogging. Blogs are an especially powerful way to engage your customers and keep you in the front of their consciousness as they go about their daily activities.

If you provide valid information that they can use on a daily basis, they will trust you and they will grow to expect and look forward to your posts every week or every two weeks or however often you post. This will also help you to keep from being put on their back burner.

Being put on a client's back burner is a sure fire way to be forgotten. There's no easier way to be forgotten than to stop reaching out to your customers. Out of sight, out of mind!

Blogging not only alleviates this, but keeps you specifically in the forefront of their mind so that when a problem arises, you're the first one they think of and they come running to you.

Spend Money! *(when appropriate)*

Alright, now let's talk about reducing your cost by spending money. That's right, you can save money by SPENDING it!

Now that may not make sense at first, but hear us out. Let's revisit one of our points from earlier: Reducing Time. Pay an expert - they charge higher rates but they do the work very fast. Allocate money for an expert to handle their field. Don't spend your time and your money, which time is money, on something in which you're not an expert. Have somebody else to do that.

Let them handle it and you're going to be able to charge for their time anyway. You're really not out anything. You are benefiting by being able to up-charge their service costs and you're saving time because you're doing other important tasks.

So make sure that when you are spending your money, and working to find out where you SHOULD spend your money, you look at the benefits of spending it. Don't look at the cost, look at the Return On Investment (ROI)

Ask yourself the following questions.

What are the benefits of having this product? What am I losing by not having this product?

When you analyze that you are going to end up figuring out pretty easily whether or not it's a valuable item or service you're spending money on. When you spend your money on software for instance, it's going to be when there's no free alternative, or there's overwhelming **value**.

An example of this in the general business world would be QuickBooks. You could use an excel sheet and that's perfectly acceptable, but it's going to take a lot more time, more man hours for you doing it and it's going to be a headache. Then, when you actually turn it over to your tax consultant there's a lot more work involved in their process so they're going to end up charging you more because they're spending more time. It's a big mess.

Often times QuickBooks or similar software that cost some money are valuable enough that you're willing to spend money on it because it saves you money in the long run.

On the marketing side, I would say spending money on a marketing coach would definitely be worth it. That would end up saving you hundreds of thousands of dollars later on because you're not making the rookie mistakes.

Facebook ads would be another example. You could spend money on Facebook ads and you can reach the hundreds of people for $20. Not a bad ROI!

With those tools, you're spending your money shrewdly and getting a great value for the amount of money you're spending. You end up saving money and reducing your overall investment in your marketing.

Some software can save you time AND money. These are especially helpful to improving the efficiency of your marketing. One of these software is Intraspect SEO, a brand new software being launched in Fall 2015. For more information, follow the link below and keep on reading for your special gift.

www.IntraspectSEO.info

Last, but certainly not least you should spend money on **networking**. You are the face of your company and your brand. Always remember that and never take that for granted.

What people *see* is what they *feel* they are going to receive. Make sure you are out there and you are presenting yourself well. Spend money on these events.

Largest Mixer is a great event to participate in. It costs a bit of money, but it's well worth it. You are getting out there and you are working with reputable people, both in the organization and the attendees at the events. Check them out at www.LargestMixer.com.

Join your local Chamber of Commerce. Just about every city and every county has a Chamber of Commerce. Go ahead and join it. Check it out and go to the events often. Those don't cost very much at all so that's going to end up being a great benefit to you.   They are easy to find, just Google "Chamber of

Commerce *[CITY] [STATE]*" (replace with your city and state).

Consider joining an exclusive group as well that focuses on marketing, such as TEAM Referral Network founded by Kelli Holmes. As they are exclusive, those do cost money and you have to dedicate time to the meetings, but it is a golden marketing community and it is well worth the time and definitely well worth the money. Check them out at www.TEAMReferralNetwork.com.

Another great one is the Entrepreneur Revolution series presented by Mel Cutler and Success Academy. The Success Academy assist entrepreneurs in all aspects of business: everything from mindset to marketing to advanced speaking. We can't recommend them enough! www.EntreRevolution.com

"If you buy things you don't need, soon you will have to sell things you need."
-Warren Buffet

MANPOWER

Time, money and manpower make up the three elements of business that are commonly over-used to create underperforming results. How you use your manpower can easily determine the fate of your company. If you are wise in the decisions you make regarding manpower your team will run efficiently and smoothly as a business should and excel in the way you dream it can.

Take heed, the following are some of the most common mistakes that business owners make with regard to manpower. Ahead lies an opportunity to improve and inspire your use of manpower to get the results you want.

Sit close and listen carefully. Here we go!

Delegate Efficiently

Reducing your manpower takes a little bit of creativity. One great way to save on manpower is to delegate, and delegate **well**. Here are a few simple tips on how to delegate efficiently that will get your manpower down.

1. Use an Assembly Line

Use an assembly line. When cars are being made initially, they were being constructed as a whole by a few people and that wasn't sufficient. It wasn't working and they were not able to produce enough cars.

So, in 1913, Henry Ford developed a system that revolutionized the car industry. He created the Assembly Line.

He found one person who was good at a certain task and he had them do that task only. Then, found another person who was good at a different task and had them do that task only.

He would have a series of these people in an a line in different parts of the factory and each person had a task and they would work on multiple pieces at a time. Once they passed Station A, they went on the Station B to get completed in the next step. Meanwhile, Station A worked received the next piece, and the cycle repeated.

If you implement this into your business because it WILL help you. Instead of having one employee do all of the work for you or YOU do all the work for you, delegate to a few individuals and play to their strengths.

One mark of an excellent leader is to recognize the skill sets of his/her followers. Take advantage of when you have an employee who has a good eye for design. Use their eye for design and don't put them in an analytical position. Have somebody good with numbers work with the analytics and don't ever expect them to do the design. They might be *able* to, but keep them focused to get the best results!

Delegate appropriately and create an assembly line so that you have people having manageable tasks, specialized tasks.

2. Goldie Locks Expectations

Next comes with your particular industry, so this is something that you need to call the shots on. You need to sit down and think about how much you should expect from your staff.

Don't expect too much, but do not expect too little. When you expect too much the morale goes down. When you expect too little your staff gets lazy. So, find your happy medium, and work within the hours for which they are already scheduled.

If you have a full time employee, make sure that they have 40 hours of work per week. You should go through the same process as you do with yourself on how much you budget in your time. You should make sure that you are budgeting enough time for them so that they can handle the projects that go over estimated hours or emergencies or just sporadic events happening.

Make sure you don't expect too much. Also, if you have employees make sure that you provide the appropriate training for them. You can have people who are very good workers and they are experienced in their job description, but they don't go above and beyond. You expect them to go above and beyond, yes it is a good thing to expect above and beyond, however, you need to be positive that they are given the proper foundation. You need to make sure that if there is a specialty skill they need to perform, they are trained appropriately.

When you expect too little from your staff then they start to walk on you. They stop showing up on time, they don't get their projects done on time and then they end up bored.

Now imagine that these are kids in a class. Expect too much from your students you see them frustrated and their grades go down. Expect too little from them and they're not challenging themselves. They're not growing as people and they get bored again and then their grades go down. This is completely in the teacher's control, just as it is completely in your control to keep your staff motivated.

So look at it that way. These people need to have stimulation in the workplace and they need to be given a reasonable amount of work. Really be practical with them just as you would be realistic with yourself.

3. Hire Others to Do the Work

There is a recurring theme in this book you may notice: **Let others focus on your work so you can work on your focus**.

That comes right back to hiring people who are experts in their field so that you can do what you do best. Delegate appropriately, delegate efficiently. Don't assign a task to someone when they are not experienced in the product or in the field. Do NOT do that. Don't say "hey, you look like you'd be good at this, go do it." That's not going to work out. Delegate *appropriately*.

Simplify Tasks

Okay, moving right along. Next I want to talk about simplifying the tasks that you assign. This will significantly reduce manpower you need because chances are, a lot of labor time gets taken up by confusion, lack of communication, or complex systems that people have to use, or lack of systems for that matter.

Explain Tasks One Step At A Time

Every task has steps. Maybe one step, 2 steps, 1000 steps. It all depends on the task, but every task as steps.

Make sure to explain them clearly. If you are sending out a memo, use bullet points and indent the sub-bullet points. Make sure that what you are giving your employees is clear.

Also, identify the learning patterns of your employees or the people you're working with. If they are visual, provide charts. If they are auditory then set up an appointment for a meeting or a voice chat, or just a phone call, or even leave a recording on their desk. Just make it clear to them. If they're kinesthetic then they're more emotion-based, so figure out who learns what way. Once you figure that out you're going to be able to communicate to them much more efficiently.

A great book as a reference for this would be *The Wizard Within*. This book sells on Amazon.com for around $12.00. It is well worth the small investment, I promise you that!

Remove Unnecessary Steps

Next, remove unnecessary steps. Every task has steps, but some of them are not necessary. That does not mean that you get to do corner cutting. Do not do corner cutting. Do not, I repeat, do NOT sacrifice quality. Do not ever sacrifice quality. ALWAYS focus on quality and how to get to your exemplary result, faster.

However, in light of delegating appropriately and simplifying tasks, you should eliminate unnecessary steps. Now here is a big step that is often overlooked: use tools and software that you understand. There are tons and tons and TONS of software out there that are quite popular. A lot of businesses use them.

QuickBooks is one of them, but these software are somewhat complex to set up and have a little bit of a learning curve to them. Some of them are worth learning. For instance

QuickBooks is something I feel is worth learning.

However, there are free software out there, and they should be considered, but often free software is more difficult to use than paid software. This is where overwhelming value comes into play when deciding between paid or free software.

For example, let's say you have a free software and it's hard to use, and that's part of the consequence of being free. In that case it would be valuable to you to buy a commercial software that you can use easily. If the paid software is easier to use, than it's usually worth the money. If not then use free system, but keep an eye out for when there are tools and software that are easy for you to understand and get the job done. Remove roadblocks, i.e. unnecessary steps!

That is where you should be putting your money. It will save manpower which will end up saving you money and will keep your employees on task if they're not worrying about "what button am I supposed to press," "did it submit," "did it format properly," etc. If they're worrying, they are not getting their job done. Make it easy for them to do their job.

Do It The Right Way The FIRST Time

Another great way that you can reduce the amount of manpower you need in your marketing department is to do things the right way the first time. This may seem like an oversimplified explanation for something that will help your business, but it really is as simple as it seems.

Doing things right the first time is comprised of three fundamental skills that you need to have mastered in order to succeed. They are gathering the right data, reading the data analytically, and learning logic.

1. Gathering the Right Data

When you're gathering data, having the right data can make the difference between a failing marketing plan and a thriving marketing plan. Be sure that you collect data that tells you exactly what you need to know.

Oftentimes, entrepreneurs and business owners make the mistake of trying to collect all the data they possibly can and they failed to recognize which data was important and which data is extraneous and just causes confusion.

For example, if you're selling a product, be sure to collect how many sales you're making. Your products can have the attention of the entire world, but if that attention isn't converting in sales it doesn't mean ANYTHING.

Now if you're selling a product, measuring how much attention your product is getting is important, but how will you know what percentage of your prospects turn into clients? This is your conversion rate, which I will demystify shortly.

You also may not need to know certain types of data. If you're part of an international company you want to know exactly where your clients are coming from, but if you're a local restaurant it doesn't matter so much where your clients are coming from as long as they come into your restaurant to get some food.

Now there are few types of data that are useful for all business types. These will help you to track exactly what you need every time. These types of data are conversions, users from your website, and leads per sale ratio. Now those may sound confusing at first, but I'm going to explain each and every one of them.

Conversions are the people that change from viewing your product or service to purchasing your product or service. This is the ratio of how many people view your product or service, and how many of those people actually convert to purchasing your product or service.

This is very important because this statistic tells you exactly how profitable your marketing plan is. It will also help you determine if you're spending more than you're making on your marketing plan, or if it's returning a profit like it should be.

Users on your website determines how much attention you're getting. This shows how many people know your company exists.

This is especially important for young startup companies. They need to know exactly how many people know about them, as that is one of the large struggles of having a young company.

As you gain users on your website you should be able to see more conversions as you go along. That's very important. As I said before, you can have the attention of the entire world and if they don't convert into sales it doesn't mean a thing.

Now, the leads per sale ratio is a little bit different from conversions, so it is important to track it separately. Leads per sale is how many leads it takes for every sale you make.

Let's say that 5 people come into your restaurant and only one of them sits down to order a meal. This means that your lead to sale ratio is 5 - 1. Out of 5 people that came in the restaurant only one sat down.

This information can help you to improve the effectiveness of your marketing plans. Not necessarily how many people you are reaching, but it will improve how many of the people you are reaching *actually partake* in your services.

This is a very important thing to know for any growing business because this will tell you, especially if you're a local business, if you're having any problems with internal staff when you're not looking, or if your company is doing great and thriving the way it should.

2. Read Data Analytically

Once you've gathered all the right data, make sure that you read your data analytically. Be very careful not to inject your emotions and your own statistics. This has led countless businesses down the path to failure simply because they refused to see when, where and how their marketing plan needs to be adjusted.

Data doesn't lie and you should treat it as truth always. That being said, there are always different interpretations of data. Make sure to analyze your data logically and in a straightforward manner.

This will keep you on the right track to success. As a rule of thumb, be certain your marketing decisions would make sense to a 5th grader and also make sure that you have based all of your marketing decisions on the data that you have collected. This will help your business to grow and to expand through a well-balanced marketing plan.

3. Learn Logic

Now that you have gathered your data and read it analytically, you need to be able to apply logic to your data to come up with a reasonable solution to whatever marketing problem or puzzle you may face.

Logic is the basic foundation upon which marketing is built. You can use your logic and reasoning skills to collect the right data, analyze it and create a simple solution. Make sure that your solution is simple. If it is complicated, it will most likely fail. Simple solutions are usually the most beautiful and effective solutions.

Now, I've said to use logic, but don't throw away your emotions and become a Vulcan. Your emotions can sometimes help you to judge a prospective client and determine the satisfaction of your client to your product or service.

Simply make sure to reason simply and carefully on crafting your marketing plan and you will be much more likely to succeed than those who don't.

"Honesty is a very expensive gift. Do not expect it from cheap people."
-Warren Buffet

PART TWO: REUSE

Why should you have to reinvent the wheel?
You can use any old wheel you like. It's already
been invented. Someone's already done that
for you. Why, then, are you reinventing
marketing?

Successful marketing is nothing new. As a
matter of fact, the knowledge you have now
regarding successful marketing has most likely
been gifted to you by either a book like this one
or by an experienced individual. This goes to
show that success in marketing is something
that can be replicated.

In this section of Reduce, Reuse, and Recycle,
we are providing you with a guide to become
more successful in your marketing endeavors.
The resources you have access to in the
following pages have assisted many

entrepreneurs like you to rise to their full potential and develop highly successful businesses.

Now it's your turn to gain access to the resources that make seven figure companies possible. Are you excited?

MARKETING GOODS

What are marketing goods you ask? They can be physical flyers, brochures, business cards, newsletter booklets, and calendars, or they can be digital marketing pieces that are viewed on a website, blog, or an email.

They are key elements to your marketing and creating a lasting impression on your target audience. Marketing goods can be costly, however, so we'll go through a few ways to cut down on the cost while still influencing your customers.

When you're looking at reusing marketing goods, think about what's best for your client. If you have clients who like physical items being sent to them, they will like getting postcards or flyers, so cater to that. If they like getting emails, cater to that. You will want to do a mixture of strategies so you're going to want to anchor people from their online experience to offline tactile items that lead them back to your online presence, etc.

When you do use physical marketing goods, ALWAYS look at how you can reuse them. For instance, you can use a flyer and design it in such a way that when it is folded, all you have to do is tape it and put a stamp on it and you can mail it to someone. No envelope needed!

That is going to be a good way to keep your costs down and you can reuse or repurpose the materials you have. So you're cutting down on your costs, you're cutting down on the materials, you're being eco-friendly and you're going to keep your brand consistent. People appreciate that.

When customers see consistency they see you as a trustworthy authority. If you're inconsistent, then that starts transitioning them into being suspicious of whether or not you can actually handle the job or the services. Or anything else that they might be purchasing from you, for that matter.

One thing that I would highly recommend is to at least integrate an E-blast system. Physical items will not be replaced.

There are theories out there saying that in a certain number of years there aren't going to be physical items, there aren't going to be business cards, there aren't going to be flyers. Well, it might be reduced quite a bit, but there's still a hefty amount of the population (and there always will be) who like tactile items; they like to feel things in their hands.

They like to see it up close. They'd rather see it in their palms than see it on the screen, but that's not very cost effective for you. So the best way to reuse these goods that are physical is to scan them into your computer or recreate them on your computer and send out a newsletter, have a blog, and reuse your marketing materials digitally.

You are expanding how many people you will reach this way. On top of that, you are reusing your brand efficiently, which helps to promote your products and services to future customers.

Also on the topic of reusing your branding, you still want to reuse your colors, your logos, your shapes, your lines and your taglines *consistently* on every item that leaves your company. That goes for business cards, that goes for newsletters, that goes for brochures, that goes for any emails that you put out, EVERYTHING under your signature in your email.

Across the board, ALWAYS stay consistent. Reuse your marketing goods; this will make your brand appear professional and organized.

To recap, reuse your physical materials, and make SURE they are dual purpose materials. As Alton Brown says "you should never have a uni-tasker."

Integrate an e-blast system. Don't rely solely on your physical goods. Use this in addition to your physical marketing materials, and it will help anchor people to your business.

Reuse logos or colors or anything else that is consistent amongst your brand. Reuse it on everything that goes out to your customers whether it's digital or physical.

"If it can't be reduced, reused, repaired, rebuilt, refurbished, resold, recycled, redesigned, or composted, then it should be restricted, redesigned, or removed from production"
-Pete Seeger

SUCCESSFUL IDEAS

Have you ever looked at a square block and wondered "Now, how can I make that roll?" No! Because you did not reinvent the wheel. It is human nature to pay attention to authorities and mentors as we grow up and learn from their successes as well as their mistakes. But once we reach a certain level of maturity, our focus turns to the task at hand rather than spending time learning from others.

Research Others in Your Field

Learning from others is a vital aspect of successful business. If you search around, you will find that 99% of millionaires, especially those who became wealthy from THEIR business, have used the guidance of experienced mentors.

On that note, let's identify a few key ways you can learn from others in your specific field as well as from successful leaders in business.

In marketing you should make sure to always reuse successful ideas whether they be your ideas or the ideas of others that have become successful. It is important to perpetuate these and learn from them as you go.

One of the ways you can do this is to research what has worked for others in your field. Your goal when analyzing your industry is to build a customer profile. You need to find out who your industry's customers are. Many times businesses (perhaps your competitors) are successful simply due to the fact that they target the right audience.

And every industry's customers are different. You don't often see florists & gear manufacturers sharing the same client base. Well, you might see that, but it is likely that one of them isn't making much money.

The good news for you there is that there are more than 7 billion people in the world, which leaves you with a seemingly endless supply of customers. Be wary though. Like I said, your industry's customers are unique. Don't market to someone else's customers. Find your own. Use surveys. Call your current clients. Do whatever you can to find out what your ideal clients are and pursue them.

Most importantly, don't market to everyone. When you market to everyone, you are marketing to no one. When you try to market to over 7 billion people, your message gets lost in a sea of advertisements that floods their perceptions every day. Make sure that you hone in on the people you really want in order to get the results you need.

Just as important as knowing who your industry's customers are, you should also find out who are *not* your industry's customers.

You can easily weed out the majority of the 7 billion people in the world and still have a plethora of clients choose from . This will help you to focus on exactly the right kind of customer for your business.

In addition, having the right kind of customer for your business will help you to succeed AND to be happy about the business you are doing.

You should also research what your successful competitors are doing. Your successful competitors are clearly doing something right; after all they *are* successful.

Find out what they're doing and model after it (as long as you can morally and legally do so without incurring copyright infringement or the like). Model success, this will help you propel yourself into their playing field and even beyond.

As you learn what makes a marketing campaign successful, it can also help you learn more about your competitors' companies and how to contend with them in the marketplace, in a respectful and proper manner.

Keep a Notebook

Another great way to promote successful ideas and reuse them in marketing is to keep a notebook of theories and ideas from successful people in marketing. Keep this notebook of theories from successful people REGARDLESS of their field and how it relates to you. The intended application by these successful people may not be the way you apply their theories to your business. An example of this is The Art of War, by Sun Tzu, a highly recommended book. As you glean by the title, this book is about war strategies, however, the concepts are profound and can be used in business and marketing strategies. Keep that in mind as you study.

In addition to The Art of War, by Sun Tzu, a great resource I have been privileged to use to increase my knowledge of marketing is The Big

<u>Boom</u> by Mel Cutler. Be creative and you will find unorthodox resources that will give you a significant competitive edge.

I have used these, and many others, taking small bits and pieces from each resource to create what I know about business and marketing success now.

Take these resources and as you go, model their excellence. Each successful person has a special niche or a special skill. Figure out what that niche or skill is and do it like them. Later, exceed what they did by evolving their techniques to fit your business and your skill sets.

If Ain't Broke, Don't Fix It
until the market changes, of course

The last way to promote successful ideas in your marketing campaign is to find ideas that work for you and keep doing it. At least for a while, that is.

Success, it is very important to note, can be replicated. No one person or class holds a unique holding over success. You can learn from the successful, as well as from the unsuccessful. You can learn to model the successful and to avoid the unsuccessful habits that some individuals have, and when you do find a technique that works for you and your marketing plan, keep doing it. That is, at least until right *before* the market changes.

You need to make sure that you change slightly ahead of the market every time the market takes a twist or a turn. The market is a roller coaster ride and by staying slightly ahead of the curve you will allow yourself the luxury of continued and successful business even when times get tough. Don't react to the changing market, BE the change in the market.

This is what makes the difference between companies that do well in poor economies and companies that do poorly in poor economies. Believe it or not, a business can do extraordinarily well in a poor economy. You want to make sure that you business not only survives, but *thrives* no matter what part of the roller coaster the economy is on. Up, down, or loop-de-loop.

"The greatest education in the world is
watching the masters at work."
-Michael Jackson

DATA

Data is possibly the most important aspect in marketing. There is no marketing without data. At all. Ever.

Marketing without data would be like driving car with no steering wheel. Sure, you can stomp your foot on the gas pedal, but you will have no control over where you're going and no idea of what is coming.

Data provides directions to keep you focus on exactly what your marketing needs to be and what it needs to not be. There are three critical categories of data you can reuse over and over again to achieve great results. They are Google Analytics, newsletter subscription information, and first hand surveys.

Pay attention to each of these types of data, as knowing how to use them correctly can transform your business forever.

The Human Brain

Ok, before we tackle the details with Google Analytics, newsletters, social media and surveys, we need to get a foundation on how the human brain works.

The human brain needs to see at least 7 impressions of a brand before it remembers it. These 7 different instances of contact need to be made with your customer before they will remember and retain your company.

These 7 steps of contact can involve any of the five senses, or methods of perception - sound, sight, touch, smell, and taste.

Imagine you are buying a car. As you drive your old car to the dealership, you see a billboard with your new car on it. You see your new shiny, sleek, black sedan. You sit in the driver's seat and feel the leather steering wheel. That brand new car smell makes you feel elite. You turn the key in the ignition, and the sound of the roar makes your hair stand on end. While waiting to sign the paperwork, they give you some cookies to eat - mmm they taste good. You <u>feel</u> the keys in your hand and you feel great!

This is part of their marketing and making the sale. It is your job to create an environment that uses as many senses as possible to engrain your brand into their subconscious.

Google Analytics

Google Analytics tracks a lot of data. Too much data. It is difficult sometimes to search through it but there are a few important actions you need to understand you can do with Google Analytics.

Track Conversions

The first action is to track conversions. We've already talked about conversions and how they're important. So to recap quickly, they will allow you to track the success of your marketing plan by showing you the ratio between how many people are looking at your product in comparison to how many people are buying it.

Remove the Spam Entries

Another godsend action you can do in Google Analytics is stop all the spam entries that routinely plague online data. As I said before, data doesn't lie but people sometimes do. Keep spammers from increasing their Google ranking and corrupting your data.

Sometimes in Google Analytics you can get an accumulation of entries that are not real, they have been generated by computer programs to entice you to buy into a product or service that is created and sold by a third party. This can be filtered out in a few ways so you can make sure your data can be correct and accurate.

Here are my top three recommendations:

1. Filter by IP Address

One of the way you can sort out these computer programs is by IP address. If you have a repeat offender who has implanted a program that gives you false readings, then you can block their IP address and thus relieve the problem.

2. Filter by Location

Another way to filter is by location. Let's say all of your business is from the United States. You can filter out the rest of the world's traffic because the traffic you WANT to see is coming from the United States. This helps remove extraneous data that gets in your way.

So what you can do is set Google Analytics to show you only updates from the United States. That will keep third party spammers from getting into your account and showing you data that isn't true.

3. Filter by Referrer

The last great way to filter data that I will cover is by referrer. If you have one particular person or website that keeps referring fake leads to you, you can block them specifically.

Because they are referring the traffic to you, they leave an imprint on your Google Analytics. You can simply block all messages from that one imprint, and voila, no more spammy junk!

For more information on how to use these filters, visit our blog:
www.deSpaindeSigns.com/blog

Project Your Growth Rate

Another important action Google Analytics allows you to do is project your growth rate. The growth rate of the company is exactly what it sounds like. It's the amount of growth that your company undergoes during a certain range of time in the future.

Your company's growth rate can be projected by using Google Analytics data from a specific time period.

If you want to know how many more visitors are going to have on your website next month than you did this month, figure out a pattern. How many additional visitors did you get between the last 3 months? Average these out and you'll come up with how many more visitors you should have *next* month.

Here is an example of a rough projection:

> Sept. = 1,000 visitors
> Oct. = 1,400 visitors
> Nov. = 2,000 visitors
>
> October is up 400 from September, and November is up 600 from October. Now add them, and then divide by the number of months you added (in this case, 2).
>
> 400 + 600 = 1,000
>
> 1000/2 = 500
>
> So, in this example, you can project that you should increase your visitor count by 500 in the month of December.

If your amount of visitors next month doesn't match, or at least get close to that number, you know that something has changed drastically.

Newsletter Subscription Data

A reliable way you can track information is by using newsletter subscription information. Don't just collect email addresses, you need a lot more information than that to successfully market to your leads. Collect phone numbers, addresses, names, and positions in the company. The rest of the details you want to extract from your leads are unique to your field.

This can help you sort out your leads and reach out to your customers in ways other than just email. Whether you need information filled out on surveys or you just want to keep them engaged with your company, newsletter subscription information is an invaluable resource for marketers.

Use your newsletter to get your 7 forms of contact with your leads. If you know from your data that your audience likes to cook Italian food, and you are primarily a cook book company, send out free recipes. That will get them to see, smell and taste your product. The visuals on your newsletter will help them remember your brand.

There are certain ways that you can engage their senses online and create your 7 forms of contact. Using social media is one of these ways.

When you use social media in conjunction with your other marketing strategies like email, phone calls, and Internet ads and whatever else you have up your sleeve, you can achieve these seven levels of contact and leave a lasting impression on your customers.

Yet another way you can use your newsletter subscription information is to nurture leads. You have to understand as an entrepreneur and a business owner that simply because someone is not interested in your product or service RIGHT NOW, doesn't mean they never will be.

You must nurture your leads with emails or content marketing to keep them thinking about you. When a problem arises that your company can solve, they will think of you first and they will seek you out and ask you for your services. You'd be surprised how many cold leads turn into customers for simple systems like these.

Physical Surveys

Another form of data you should be certain to incorporate into your marketing is physical first hand surveys.

The importance and need for customer feedback cannot possibly be overstated. Customer feedback is by far the best and most accurate way to find out what your customers want and what they need and how satisfied they are with your service or product. This can help you to improve your product so that more people buy your product and your service.

You should also use physical first hand surveys to conduct market research. Use surveys, email or whatever you can to find out what your customer's pain is.

Find out what they most desperately need and what they desperately want to improve in their business, then provide the solution. Find the pain, and BE the solution. Position your product or service as the solution to their problem. This will paint you as an expert and you will have people begging for your services and products.

"Data by itself is useless. Data is only useful if you apply it."
-Todd Park

PART THREE: RECYCLE

How long do you keep leftovers in the refrigerator? Be honest, is it a day? A week? Since last June? After a while, it is appropriate to throw your leftovers into the recycle bin. Marketing strategies are no different.

Oftentimes entrepreneurs find a strategy that works, they use it and continue to use it long after it doesn't work anymore.

You are not that entrepreneur. You learn to recycle strategies and stay ahead of the curve. You know that this gives you a critical edge over your competitors.

In the recycle section of Reduce, Reuse, and Recycle you will learn that old strategies should be retired and recycled. We will share with you the dangers of pushy marketers and what you should replace them with to increase your marketing success.

Ready?

Good.

OLD STRATEGIES

Your marketing strategies should be ever changing with the ebb and flow of society. Your clients are evolving, so should you.

An old strategy can be 20 years old or 1 week old. The old strategies are purely the ones that obviously don't align with your mission and goals. Assuming that part of your mission and goals is to reach your target audience, the strategies that are not getting you that result should be recycled.

In marketing it is very important to be able to recycle old strategies. When it's not working anymore it's time to go. Staying two steps ahead of the market will mean you have to adapt new strategies and put the old ones in the recycle bin.

Markets change. In addition, they, especially digital markets, change very fast. In many cases, the strategy will only work for a certain time period. The range of time depends on the market and your strategy. Sometimes even as quickly as a matter of days.

Be flexible. The more flexible and adaptable you are to your surroundings, the better you and your business will survive.

For example, when Priceline began as a startup company in the late 90's, the travel industry was changed forever. The travel industry was decimated because the rest of the travel companies did not keep up with the change fast enough.

What Priceline did that no other company had done before is allow their customers to compare travel prices online at their personal computers.

Now, many of the travel companies that already existed were counting on people not being able to search around and they charged higher prices because of it. When Priceline came around and created a platform on which price and availability comparison can be done easily and quickly, the travel market was decimated and changed forever.

Now a number of companies have followed Priceline's example, and the travel market is much more competitive than it used to be. All travel agencies now have to compete with each other's prices instead of being restricted by location.

This is just one example of how market can change in a heartbeat. Be aware of the changes in your market. Make sure that you're two steps ahead of them at all times so that you can be the one to take your clients to the next level of your industry.

"The measure of intelligence is the ability to change."
"The definition of insanity is to do the same thing over and over again and expect a different result."
-Albert Einstein

BAD MARKETING STAFF

Your marketing campaign is the face of your business to those who don't yet know your business clearly. This means it is crucial to ensure your marketing staff is made up of the type of people you would WANT to have representing your business.

The pushy tactics that marketers have used in the past are not only no longer effective, but they WILL hurt your businesses image. We will now talk about three of the most dangerous types of marketers: the used car salesman, the snake oil salesman, and the bump on a log.

As your marketing plans progress, watch out for these guys in your marketing staff.

Marketing is very much sales and sales is marketing. Those are the two pillars of your business, but what happens when you have a bad marketing staff.

Well, you don't even get to the sales process. We have outgrown the used car salesman. Back when they would say "There's no better time to buy used car but you'd better hurry because they're gone, they're GONE," it worked.

Now, we have outgrown that; we are too smart for that. We look at these salesmen and marketers and we see slime. We see "Uh I can NOT trust that person."

You want to project trust; you want to project knowledge. You want to touch the minds of these people and their emotions without selling them a used car and trying to cover up that the brake pads haven't been replaced in 20 years.

So if you have the used car salesman approach, get rid of it. Recycle it to somewhere else. Throw it in the garbage disposal. I'm serious, GET RID of the used car salesman approach. People don't like it, and people don't trust it. You need to develop trust, that is extraordinarily important.

Let's say someone came up to you and said "Hey here's this car and it's got brand new paint and brand new this and brand new tires and brand new handles and everything else but the engine's missing." Would you buy that car?

Absolutely not, and if you would, you shouldn't be running a business. You have to change how you approach your customers. If people are not trusting you, you need to change your approach and how you're talking to them. How you're presenting yourself to them.

Get rid of the of the non-transparent approach, you must always be transparent. You must always be honest. You don't necessarily have to say everything, you don't need to get into all the detail, but don't shove things in people's faces. If they want your services and you presented well they will come to you.

The cousin to the car salesman is the snake oil salesman. This is a slightly different approach than the used car salesman uses. The used car salesman is hiding things and pushing things in people's faces and expecting them to buy just because you being pushy.

Snake oil is just lying. It's like having this tonic that is supposed to grow your hair and you sell it to the person and they come back and it's not working at all because you didn't use this other stuff so let me sell that to you. Well, same as the used car salesman, this doesn't work. So, needless to say, you should not be taking this approach.

That's just dishonesty. Snake oil salesmen are simply dishonest. So look at honesty. If your staff is doing this to YOUR customers and leads, get rid of them. Just flat out, they cannot be trained. If they're doing this, it's too ingrained in their souls to be trained out.

Just remove them and replace them with people who have the ability to be sincere and honest and be able to sell something to someone because they understand the need.

The difference between the good marketing and bad marketing usually is the intent. Good marketing is based on feeling a need in resolving a pain. Bad marketing is based on dollar signs.

If you're doing your job and you're feeling the pain, you're removing the issues that are in the lives of your clients, and money will come. If you are focusing on the dollar sign and just pushing products to people that are never going to use them, it doesn't work; it's not going to bring you any money.

You can get one client, one time, but they're not going to return to you. It's just not going to happen. Marketing used to work like that, but it doesn't work like that anymore. So if you have a snake oil salesman on your staff, put down this book or press stop on the recording and go fire them right now. It's hurting your business.

The next type of salesman may be very honest, and may mean well, but they don't follow through. This is the bump on the log salesman.

You can have an amazing product and you can have a wonderful staff and you can have the best client that give you money, but when you have marketing staff that is all talk and no results, they don't follow through and give you the leads, they don't follow through and make sure that whatever your system needs they give to you.

If they're supposed to give information to your developers or your writers or the contractors or anything like that, and they're not giving that information over properly then that's useless information. They might mean well they might be good people, but they're not doing their job correctly.

So to fix this, this person might be trainable. They need an incentive, this might come back to when we talked about expecting the right amount from your employees. Don't expect too much and don't expect too little and too little has been expected of this employee.

So they are bored, they don't have consequences, maybe they don't have a system to follow. You need to step it up as a manager with the bump on a log salesman.

You can you get rid of the other guys flat out, and you can step it up as a manager to help this person become their full potential. These steps will allow you marketing staff to function as a cohesive unit, and successfully bring in new customers.

> "A bad attitude is like a flat tire...you can't
> go anywhere until you change it."
> -Unknown

IN THE BOX MARKETING

Times have changed, and so has marketing. It's now time to recycle "in the box" marketing. There are far too many channels for consumers to receive products or services for the old used car salesman tactics to work.

Don't be pushy; you won't be doing anybody any favors by shoving your product at them. Instead, create relationship with your customers. This will create rapport with your customers and make repeat customers that are loyal to you and your brand.

There are a few styles specifically that have changed from the old style marketing.

1. Direct Mail

First is direct mail. Most people get so much junk mail these days that they don't even check what it is. They simply throw it away, never opening it, and that's marketing dollars in the trash can, literally in the trash can.

2. Guilt Trips

The next tactic that needs to change is guilt trips. Many years ago companies would try to guilty people into purchasing their product. Whether by pure peer pressure (as with the cigarette industry), or by creating a situation where I feel guilty if I don't buy the product or service.

That doesn't work anymore. This violates your relationship with the customer, and diminishes the trust and rapport between you and your customer.

Instead of enforcing these techniques, create a unique experience with your customer. Give them something extra that they won't get with anyone or anywhere else. Create an experience, not just a service or product. This tactic will bring your business a competitive edge over your competitors, and your company will be set up for success!

"Instead of thinking outside the box, get rid of the box."
-Deepak Chopra

THANK YOU!

Thank you for reading our book! We hope this helps you get started on your road to successful marketing! Please follow us on FaceBook, Twitter, Instagram, Pinterest, and LinkedIn, check out our blog and join our newsletter for more nuggets of marketing wisdom.

As promised, here is your special gift!

50% off our new software
Intraspect SEO
for one year!

To opt-in, go to IntraspectSEO.info and join the other soon to be successful entrepreneurs!

RESOURCES

- Largest Mixer
  www.LargestMixer.com

- ScreenLight for video production
  www.ScreenLight.tv

- TEAM Referral Network
  www.TEAMReferralNetwork.com

- Entrepreneur Revolution presented by
  Success Academy
  www.EntreRevolution.com

- The Big Boom, by *Mel Cutler*
  www.BigBoomBook.com

- The Art of War, by *Sun Tzu*

- The Wizard Within, by *A. M. Krasner*

ABOUT THE AUTHORS

Jennifer de Spain, soon to be Jennifer Robertson, is CEO and founder of deSpain deSigns, a California Corporation focused on custom web design and online marketing strategies. She has had a passion for website development since she attended Mt. San Jacinto College, where she graduated with a 4.0GPA in Multimedia with an emphasis in web design. She continues her independent education to provide the best quality service and products for her wonderful customers.

Timothy Robertson is currently Chief of Marketing at deSpain deSigns, a California based web design and online marketing company. He has been involved with marketing and web design companies for over eight years. He graduated in June 2015 with an A.S. in Engineering Technology, as well as a certification in Engineering Graphics, and is currently attending California Polytechnic State University in Pomona in pursuit of a B.S. in Manufacturing Engineering.